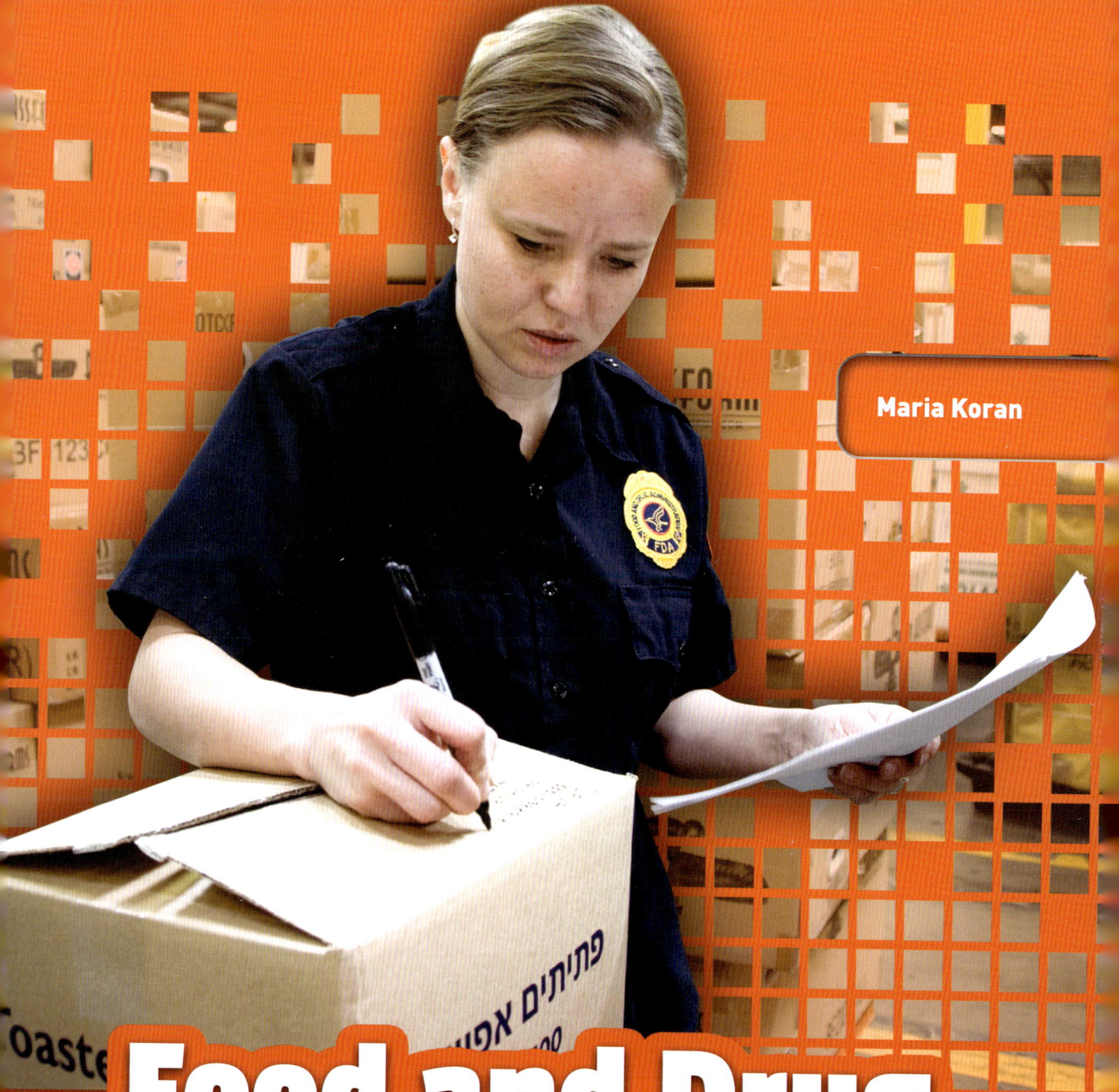

Maria Koran

Food and Drug Administration

POWER • AUTHORITY • GOVERNANCE

LIGHTBOX
openlightbox.com

Go to
www.openlightbox.com
and enter this book's
unique code.

ACCESS CODE

LBXN8899

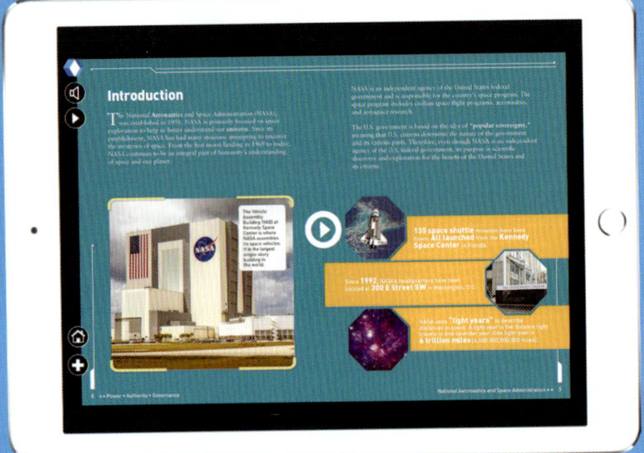

Lightbox is an all-inclusive digital solution for the teaching and learning of curriculum topics in an original, groundbreaking way. Lightbox is based on National Curriculum Standards.

STANDARD FEATURES OF LIGHTBOX

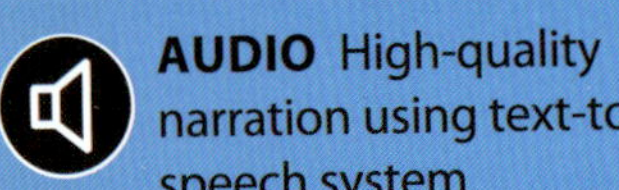
AUDIO High-quality narration using text-to-speech system

WEBLINKS Curated links to external, child-safe resources

INTERACTIVE MAPS Interactive maps and aerial satellite imagery

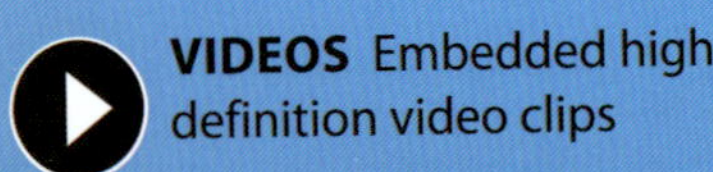
VIDEOS Embedded high-definition video clips

SLIDESHOWS Pictorial overviews of key concepts

QUIZZES Ten multiple choice questions that are automatically graded and emailed for teacher assessment

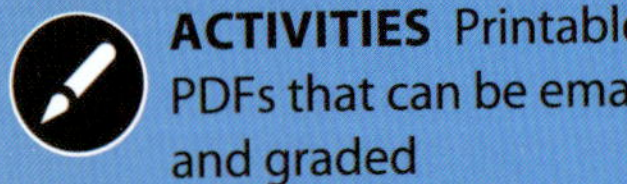
ACTIVITIES Printable PDFs that can be emailed and graded

TRANSPARENCIES Step-by-step layering of maps, diagrams, charts, and timelines

KEY WORDS Matching key concepts to their definitions

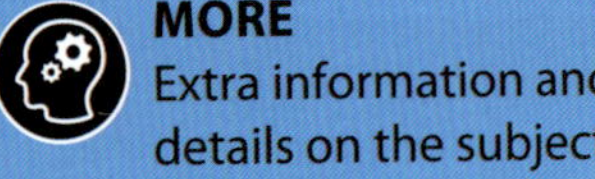
MORE Extra information and details on the subject

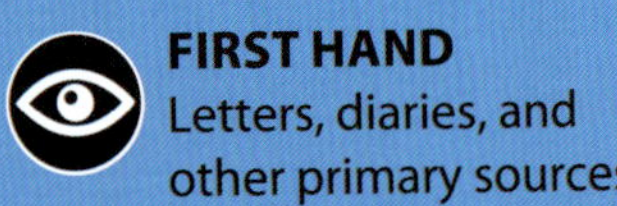
FIRST HAND Letters, diaries, and other primary sources

DOCS Speeches, newspaper articles, and other historical documents

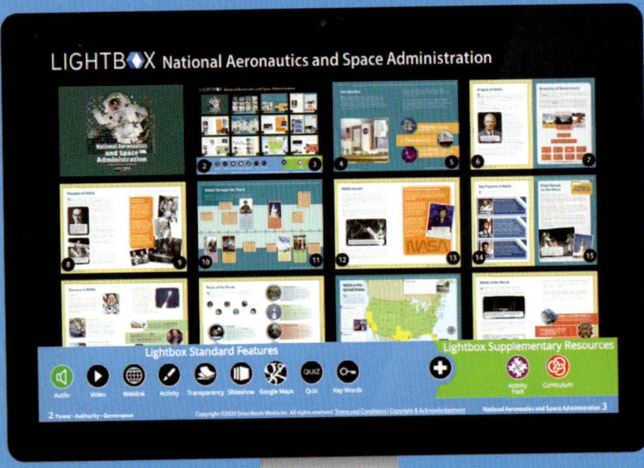

POWER • AUTHORITY • GOVERNANCE

Food and Drug Administration

CONTENTS

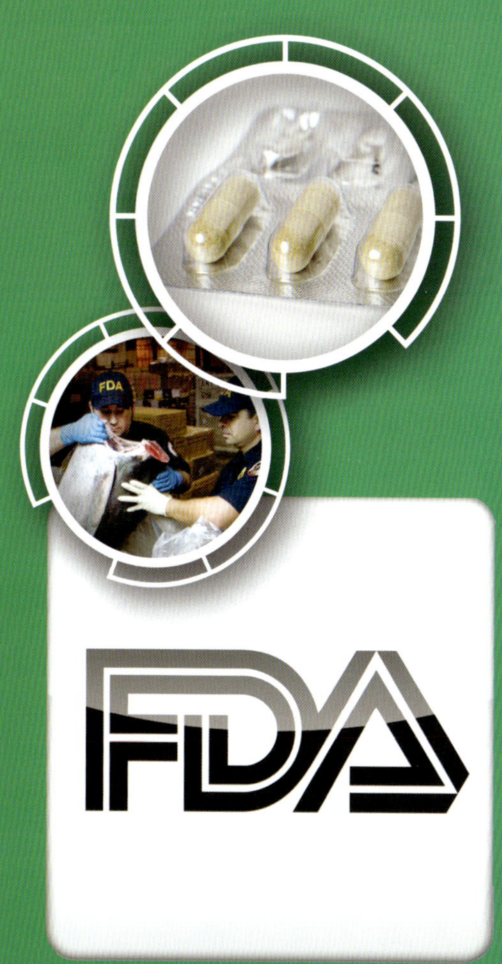

Introduction

In the early 1900s, the United States had a problem with food that was making people sick. There was also a problem with phony medicines that were sold across state lines. The United States needed an organization to take control of the situation and regulate it. That organization is today called the Food and Drug Administration (FDA).

The FDA is the organization that decides if food and medicines are safe. It is not a law enforcement agency and cannot arrest anyone. The FDA has control over medicines for both humans and animals. It also regulates tobacco and **cosmetic products**.

The FDA wants to keep people safe. It helps the Department of Homeland Security (DHS) with counter-terrorism. The FDA checks the food supply. It also helps get medicines to the public to treat wide-scale health threats.

The FDA has 223 field offices in the United States, Virgin Islands, and Puerto Rico.

The U.S. government is based on the idea of **"popular sovereignty."** The U.S. citizens give power and authority to the government. All parts of the government serve the will of the people. The FDA has great authority and power. However, even it must obey certain rules. These rules and laws come from the U.S. **Constitution**.

The FDA must be careful when inspecting food, medicine, medical equipment, cosmetics, and tobacco. Any mistake they make judging the safety of a product could be very dangerous to the public. It could take years and many legal battles to make right.

The FDA is under the direction of the **Department of Health and Human Services (HHS)**. The Department of Health, Education, and Welfare became the HHS on **May 4, 1980**.

The HHS headquarters is in the **Hubert H. Humphrey Building** in Washington, D.C. It was the **first federal building** named after a living person. Hubert Humphrey was a former U.S. Vice President.

The **U.S. Constitution** is a short document. During the late **1780s**, the Constitution was changed by adding amendments to it. The **first ten** amendments are called the **Bill of Rights**.

Origins of the FDA

The origins of the FDA go back a long way. In 1862, President Abraham Lincoln put Charles M. Wetherill in charge of the new Department of Agriculture. That led to the Bureau of Chemistry in 1901.

In 1906, President Teddy Roosevelt signed into law the Pure Food and Drugs Act. Although there had been pressure on the government for more than 25 years to ensure the safety of food and medicine in the United States, there was no single organization that was in charge of so large a task.

In 1906, author Upton Sinclair wrote a book about the terrible, unhealthy conditions in the Chicago Stockyards. The title of Sinclair's book was *The Jungle*. Chicago was the main center for meat processing and distribution in the country. When people read his book, they were shocked to learn what was going on with their food. They demanded something be done, and right away. When President Roosevelt read the book, he was outraged.

Upton Sinclair won the Pulitzer Prize for Fiction in 1943.

The Pure Food and Drugs Act passed quickly. Although the work of the agency began with the passage of the Food and Drug Act, the agency was not called the Food and Drug Administration until 1930.

Branches of Government

The Department of Health and Human Services is a Cabinet level post in the executive branch of the government. This means that the FDA reports to the secretary of Health and Human Service. Since HHS is part of the executive branch, the secretary of Health and Human Service reports to the president.

The U.S. government is organized so that no one of the three branches has unlimited power. This system is known as "**checks and balances**." The idea is that each branch can "check" the power of the other two. This gives "balance" to the government.

Congress controls the budget of HHS, and HHS has power over the FDA. Congress also has the power to investigate both.

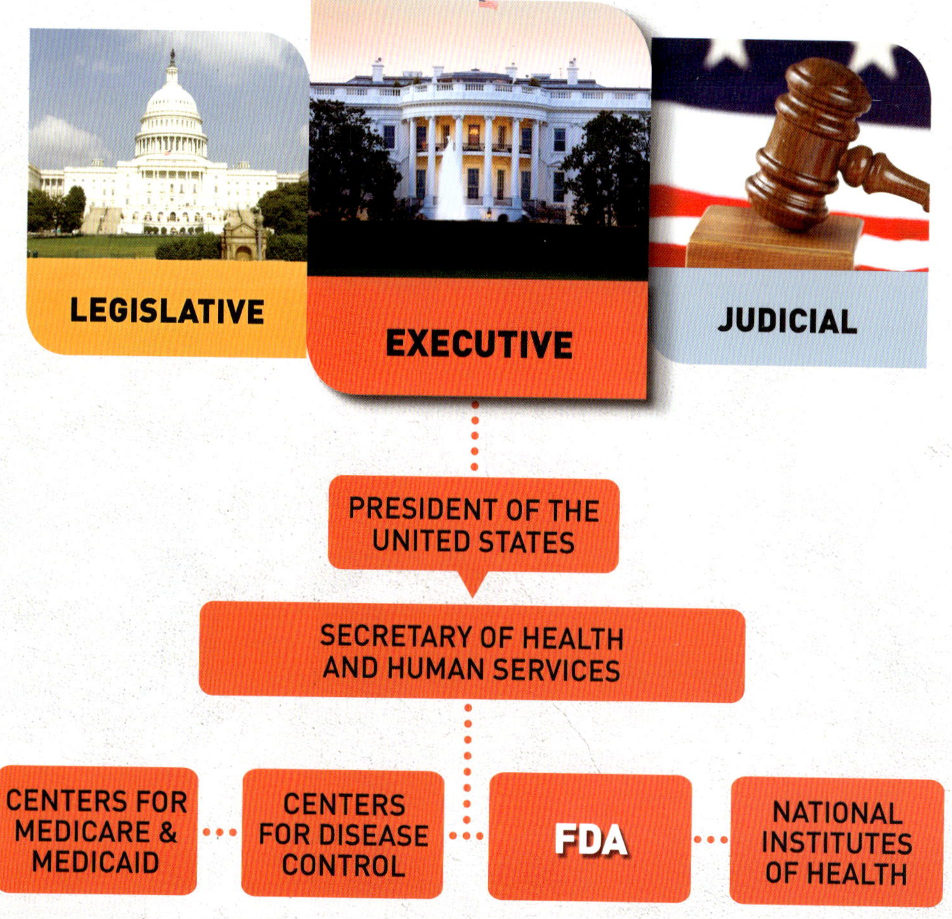

Purpose of the FDA

The FDA's job is to keep U.S. citizens safe. It protects them from many dangers. Spoiled food, dangerous medicines, faulty medical equipment, cosmetics that might harm us, and dangerous products such as tobacco are all controlled by the FDA.

The FDA is responsible for recalling contaminated food.

The FDA inspects and regulates the food supply. It decides if medical drugs are safe and effective. It makes sure that medical equipment works and is safe. It inspects cosmetics to make sure they do not emit radiation. It regulates the tobacco industry. That is a great deal of power and authority. Where does it come from?

Federal agencies are created by the executive branch. However, Congress controls who becomes the agencies' leaders. Congress also controls the agency's ability to make rules, known as **regulations.** These rules are actually laws. The Constitution only gives Congress the right to pass laws. So, it is Congress that gives the FDA its power and authority.

It is the FDA's job to keep U.S. citizens safe from many dangers. But what about personal freedom? When does the FDA cross the line and block our **civil liberties**?

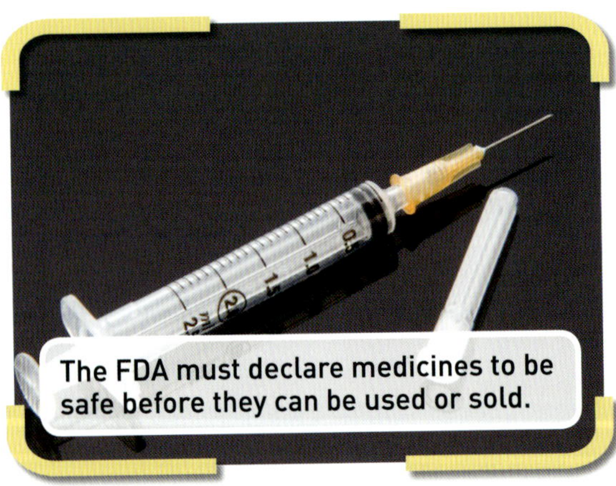
The FDA must declare medicines to be safe before they can be used or sold.

Prohibition

The United States is founded on the idea of personal freedom. The laws we make are to protect and keep us safe, not take away our freedom. But when does the intent to keep us safe break our personal freedom?

On January 26, 1919, Congress passed the **Eighteenth Amendment**. It made it illegal to make, sell, or transport alcohol anywhere in the United States. The amendment was meant to prevent people from hurting themselves with alcohol. However, it destroyed thousands of businesses. Many felt it took away the right to choose. Did the government go too far? On December 5, 1933, Congress changed its mind and **repealed** the Eighteenth Amendment. In this case, freedom of choice won over intent to protect.

The Philadelphia Inquirer

LATE CITY EDITION

PROHIBITION'S 14-YEAR RULE ENDED; PRICES HIGH, SUPPLY LOW IN PHILA

CITY 'DEAD,' REAL STUFF HARD TO GET

Liquor at $75 a Case, $6 a Pint and 50 Cents a Drink Scare off Patrons; 'Speaks' Do Usual Business; Gin, Wines Plentiful, But Not in Great Demand

MERRILY WE TOSS 'EM DOWN, TOSS 'EM DOWN

ROOSEVELT ASKS U. S. TC GUARD LAW

President's Proclamation Declarin Repeal of 18th Amendment Cal on Nation to Cherish New Fre dom; Utah's Ratification, as 36t State, Sounds Knell of Dry Era

FDA Through the Years

The FDA has been working for over 100 years to protect the health of U.S. citizens. The work done by the agency is just as important today as it was back in 1906.

June 23. 1906

The Pure Food and Drugs Act is passed. This led the way to the creation of the FDA.

June 1930

The Food, Drug, and Insecticides Organization shortens its name to today's Food and Drug Administration.

June 24, 1938

President Franklin Roosevelt signs the Food, Drug, and Cosmetic Act. This gives the FDA much more power and authority.

March 28, 1979

The Three Mile Island Nuclear power plant has a partial meltdown. Radiation is released. The FDA helps investigate possible harmful health effects.

1937

A mass poisoning of 107 people treated with an untested medication spurs Congress to empower the FDA to monitor drug safety.

June 30, 1965

Warning labels must now be placed on the outside of packs of cigarettes because of the Federal Cigarette Labeling and Advertising Act.

July 15, 1965

The Drug Abuse Control Amendment is passed to help control the use of illegal drugs.

1982

Seven people die from pain medication laced with cyanide. The nation is gripped by fear. The scare leads to new packaging laws.

January 4, 1983

The Orphan Drug Act is passed. It supports the development of cures for rare diseases, such as Lou Gehrig's Disease.

September 2006

Spinach contaminated with the *e-coli* bacteria make 199 people in 26 states sick. Three die from the illness. The FDA investigates.

June 22, 2009

The Family Smoking Prevention and Tobacco Control Act gives the FDA authority to regulate the manufacture, distribution, and marketing of tobacco products to protect public health.

December 13, 2016

The 21st Century Cures Act is passed. It is meant to get new medical products and medicines to patients who need them more quickly.

February 14, 2018

The FDA announces the approval of a new method of detecting concussions. The method, a blood test, is cheap and safe.

FDA Issues

It is the job of the FDA to protect U.S. citizens from unsafe foods, medicines, cosmetics, and tobacco. However, they are not perfect. The FDA has faced many issues.

The Affordable Care Act (ACA) requires restaurants to show the calories in their food. That way you can know how many calories are in a meal such as a double cheeseburger and fries. However, the FDA has suggested that grocery stores do the same thing. That is not what the law states. Packaged foods have that information on their labels already. Asking for more than a law requires in an example of **overreach.**

The FDA is the agency that decides if a medicine is safe and can be put on the market. However, the FDA receives much of its funding from **pharmaceutical** companies. This is a **conflict of interests.**

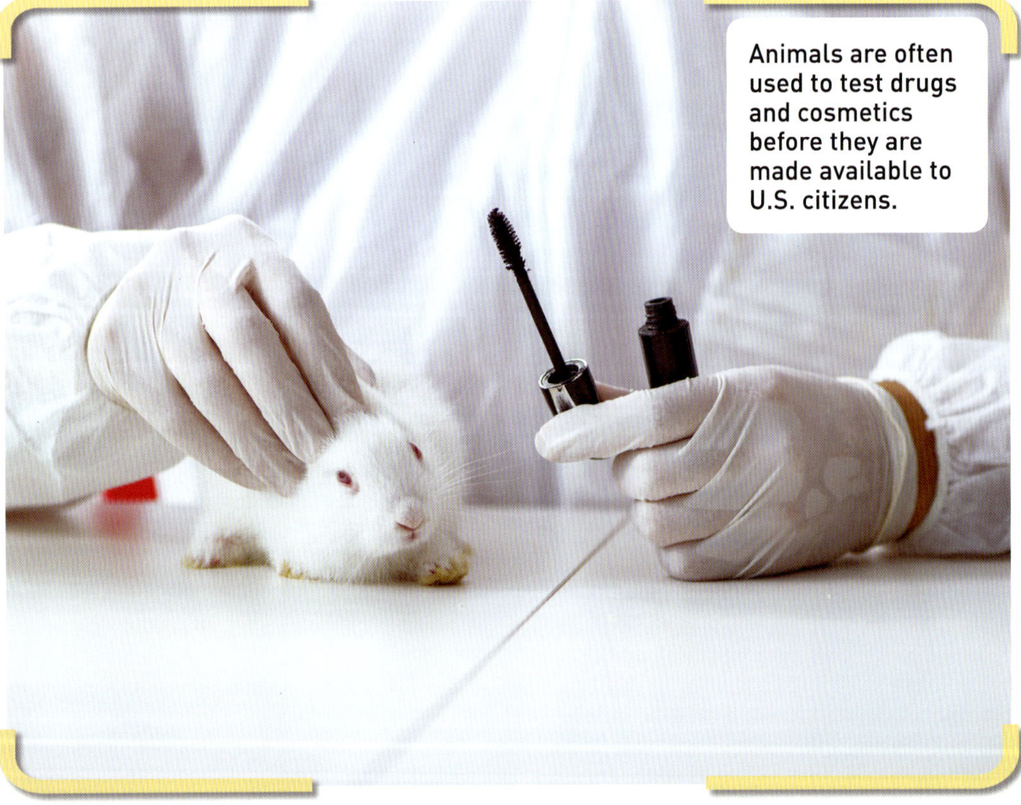

Animals are often used to test drugs and cosmetics before they are made available to U.S. citizens.

The FDA controls the cosmetics industry. For many years, cosmetic companies tested on live animals to see if their products would hurt humans. Even after they knew the results, many companies still did cruel tests on the animals. The FDA could have stopped them but did not. Today, laws have been passed that make it easier to put drugs on the market. These laws even allow for testing on humans. The FDA must balance the need to test drugs with the need to keep test subjects safe.

More Checks and Balances

It may seem as if a federal agency has unlimited power. However, this is not true. The government's system of checks and balances applies to agencies, too. The FDA is a part of HHS. HHS has the authority to check the power of the FDA.

The commissioner of the FDA in 2019 was Dr. Scott Gottlieb. He was nominated by the president and confirmed by the U.S. Senate. However, the FDA is a part of HHS, so Dr. Gottlieb had to report to Mr. Tom Price, the secretary of HHS.

The power of the FDA can also be checked by the U.S. Congress. Congress has the power to investigate the FDA. Congress also has some control over the FDA's budget. These are all checks that help stop the FDA from becoming too powerful.

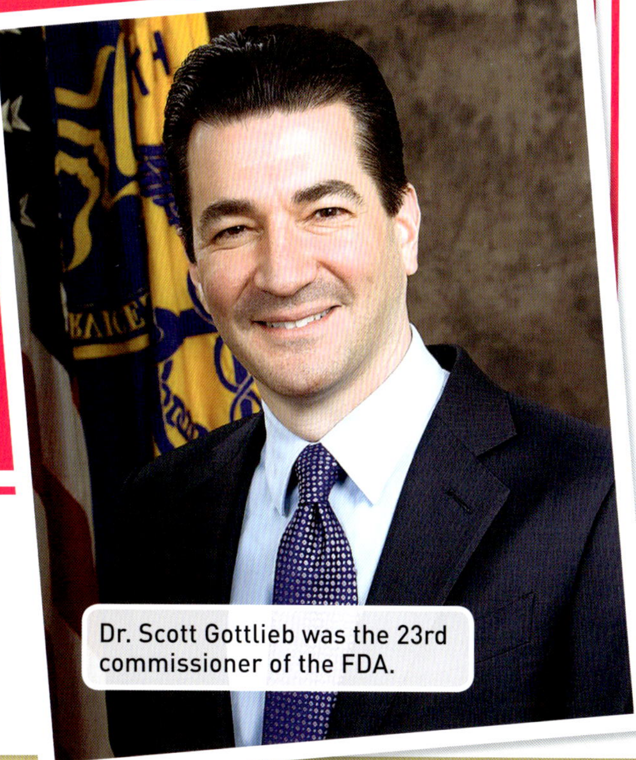

Dr. Scott Gottlieb was the 23rd commissioner of the FDA.

Key Figures in the FDA

Many notable people have made important contributions to the safety of the United States while working for the FDA. Many FDA commissioners have been important figures.

Harvey W. Wiley

Harvey W. Wiley (1844–1930) was appointed the commissioner of the Bureau of Chemistry after he wrote the Pure Food and Drugs Act of 1906. He was appointed by President Teddy Roosevelt. Wiley went on to champion safer foods in the "Better Homes and Garden" magazine.

Dr. Jane E. Henney

Dr. Jane E. Henney (1947–) was the first female commissioner of the FDA. She was appointed by President Bill Clinton. She served from 1988 until 2001. As a doctor, she was trained in oncology, which is the treatment of cancer.

Dr. Scott Gottlieb

Dr. Scott Gottlieb (1972–) was the most recent commissioner of the FDA. He served from May 11, 2017 until April 5, 2019. He is now a fellow at the American Enterprise Institute.

Harvey Wiley's Fight for Safe Food and Drugs

HISTORICAL CASE STUDY

In the 1880s, markets in the United States were filled with poor and even dangerous products. Many crooked people known as "snake oil salesmen" cheated. They altered medicines or sold strange liquids claiming they would cure everything. Instead, those fake products did nothing or harmed the people who used them.

For example, bee honey was sometimes mixed with sugar syrup. "Pure" olive oil was mixed with other oils. Many "sleeping tonics" had dangerous drugs in them. The condition of the nation's food supply was unsafe. Many people were getting sick from the food. Something had to be done.

Harvey Wiley moved to Washington, D.C. in 1883 and became the head chemist for the Department of Agriculture. During the 1880s and 1890s, Wiley wrote many bills to Congress fighting for cleaner food and drugs. None of the bills passed. Still, Wiley would not give up the fight.

In 1902, Wiley organized a widespread fight for safe food and drugs. He convinced a group of healthy young men to test food and drugs on themselves in public. People saw the harmful results. The nation had had enough. Wiley wrote the Pure Food and Drugs Act in 1906. President Roosevelt signed it into law. To reward Wiley for his tireless work, the president made him the commissioner of the new Bureau of Chemistry.

Careers in the FDA

Physicians

Doctors and physicians are some of the most important people in the FDA. Rather than working on patients, FDA physicians use their knowledge to decide if medical drugs or equipment work. They judge public health risks and often lead many teams of other FDA experts.

Health Scientist

These are the experts who decide on policies and how to put them in action. They study problems in the health care system and decide how to fix them. They are often writers who are published in respected health journals.

Program Analyst

Program analysts handle staffing needs and decide how much money each program needs to do its job. They determine the budget for each FDA program and work to keep each program running smoothly.

Animal Caretaker

The FDA is also responsible for the country's **veterinary medicine**. Animal caretakers work to feed, water, and care for the many different types of animals that the FDA uses.

The FDA's budget request to Congress in 2018 was **$5.1 billion** dollars. However, it receives most of its funding from outside sources such as fees.

The leader of the FDA is known as the **commissioner**. The position is nominated by the president but **must be** confirmed by the U.S. Senate.

STEM stands for Science, Technology, Engineering, and Math. Of the **hundreds** of careers in the FDA, **almost all** of them depend on STEM.

Tools of the Trade

The FDA requires many different types of tools and devices to do its job. Some of these tools are medical. Others include specialized gauges for measuring very small changes in equipment. Still others include common farm equipment, or even baby bottles for feeding young animals.

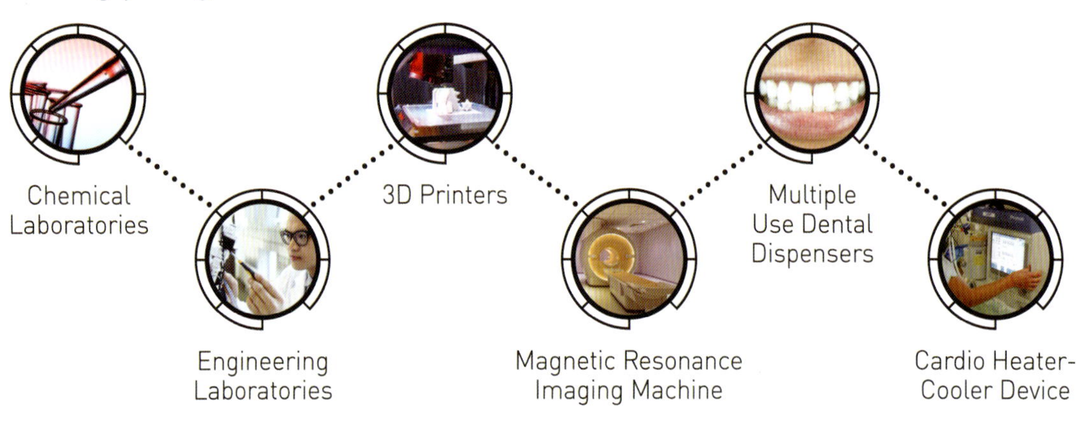

Chemical Laboratories

The FDA is responsible for making certain that food, drugs, and cosmetics are safe. Chemical laboratories are among the most important tools it has. Inside the labs, the FDA can run tests to make sure that products are safe.

Engineering Laboratories

The FDA also makes sure that medical equipment is safe to use. To do this, the agency has to run detailed engineering tests on each new product. FDA employees might take a product apart or even run destruction tests on it. Engineering labs are very important to the FDA's mission.

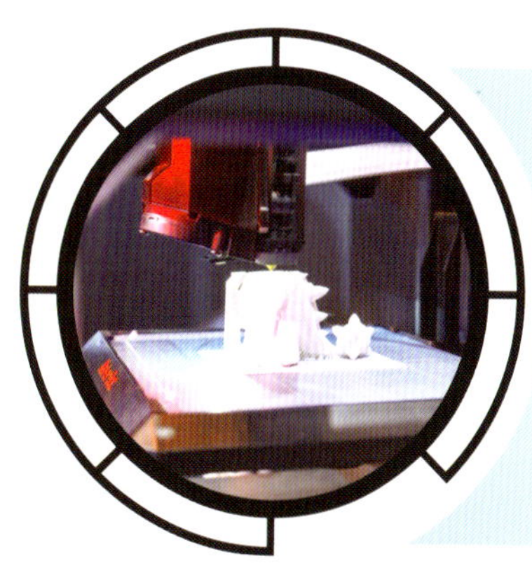

3D Printers

The FDA is responsible for making sure that packaging used for drugs and medicine is safe. The 3D printer is cutting-edge technology. A person can enter blueprints and the printer makes the item perfectly. This saves a great deal of money. Designs can be tested without spending money on building prototypes that might fail.

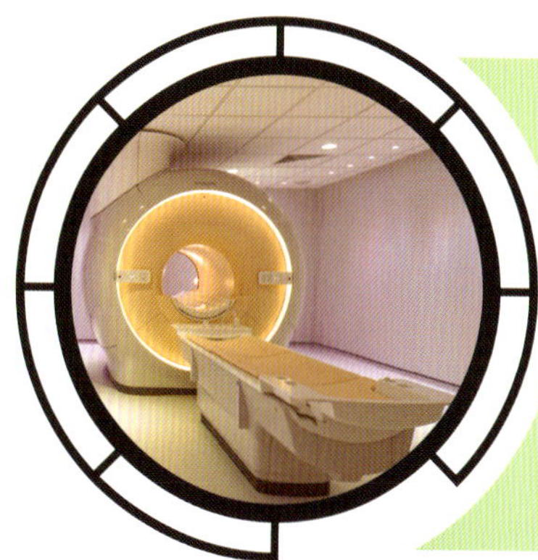

Magnetic Resonance Imaging Machine

An MRI machine is a big scanner that looks like a tube. It scans the human body. The person being scanned lies down and the scanner uses magnetic fields to get images of the inside of his or her body. This is much safer than having to cut someone open to see what is going on inside them.

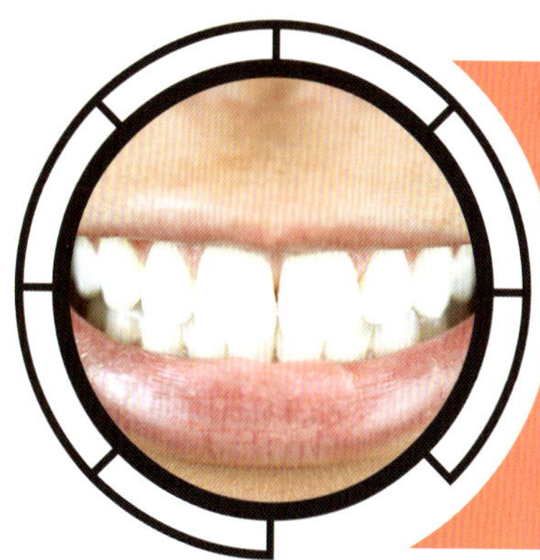

Multiple Use Dental Dispensers

Multiple Use Dental Dispensers were an invention that was tested by the FDA before being released to the public. They are syringes where the needle tip is thrown away but the dispenser can be reused many times. They save a great deal of money and have been proven to be safe. These tools are very useful for FDA testing. Many dentists also use them.

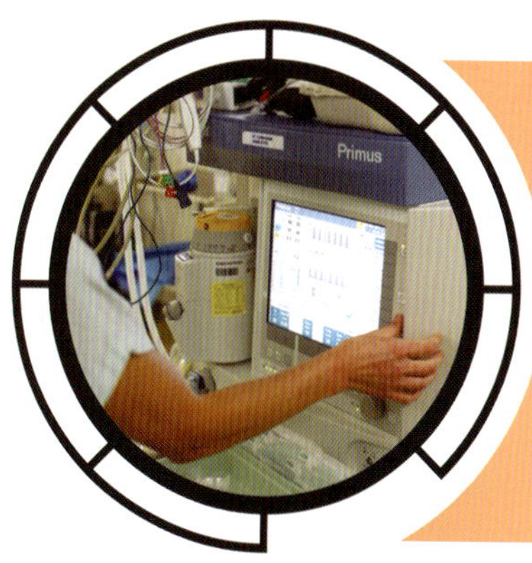

Cardio Heater-Cooler Device

This device is used during heart or lung surgery. It helps keep the patient's body either warm or cold. However, the FDA has started to test it very carefully. Some patients have become sick with a **bacterial** infection after surgery. The FDA is making sure that the machine is safe for more surgeries.

FDA in the United States

The FDA works across the United States. This means that the agency must work and cooperate with many different agencies and organizations. Of course the FDA works with other health organizations, but it also works with local law enforcement to help with investigations.

1

Atlanta, Georgia

Atlanta is the headquarters of the Center for Disease Control (CDC). The CDC was started to control communicable diseases. It began in 1946 to fight malaria, and the FDA was important in the early days of its work. The FDA and CDC still work together very often to solve mysterious illnesses all over the country.

2

Knoxville, Tennessee

In 1937, there was a mass poisoning in Tennessee. 107 people, including many children, were killed. Hundreds more across several states became very sick. The FDA was called in to investigate. The cause was discovered to be a type of fake medicine called "Elixir of Sulfanilamide." The makers claimed it cured a wide range of illnesses. But, like so many "snake oils," it killed people. The FDA worked with the FBI during the investigation. This tragedy is what gave the FDA national control over purity of medicines.

3

Love Canal, New York

Love Canal, New York, was the site of one of the worst **ecological** disasters in U.S. history. In February of 1978, this community discovered that it was built on a **toxic** waste dump site. The storage barrels rusted through. Thousands of gallons of toxic waste came to the surface. The FDA, along with many other agencies including the Environmental Protection Agency (EPA), CDC, and law enforcement, were called in to help.

4

Silver Springs, Maryland

Although the FDA has many offices in Maryland, the White Oak Campus in Silver Springs, Maryland, is the headquarters of the FDA. Many joint investigations have happened here.

FDA in the World

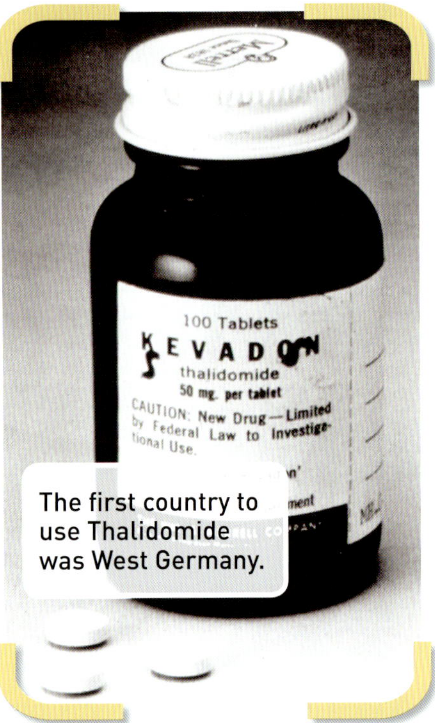

The first country to use Thalidomide was West Germany.

In 1957, a new drug was released in Europe. It was called Thalidomide. It was supposed to help pregnant women. It was released in 46 countries around the world, but not in the United States. FDA doctor Frances Kelley did not trust it. This was a fortunate refusal. Thalidomide turned into the biggest man-made medical disaster in world history.

Thalidomide caused horrible birth defects. We now know that at least 10,000 babies were born with defects. In this case, the FDA benefited from the medical information from many other countries.

The FDA has recently opened field offices across the world. There are more than 100 offices from Afghanistan to Zimbabwe. The reasons for this expansion are easy to understand. The FDA wants to protect and promote public health around the world. This is because people are traveling around the world every day. It is better to stop a global epidemic than to try and treat one.

The United States also imports much of our food from foreign countries. With offices overseas, the FDA can make sure food is safe before it reaches our shores. This is excellent international cooperation. With offices overseas, the FDA can make sure that the medical supplies we import are safe for U.S. citizens.

The FDA's Office of International Programs (OIP) works with governments in foreign countries to help assure that food and medical products exported to the United States meet U.S. standards. The OIP has offices in China, India, Europe and Latin America.

The FDA wants to stop the spread of dangerous diseases such as **Ebola**. In 2018, there were more than **500** confirmed cases of Ebola.

Nearly **40** countries have officially banned the testing of cosmetics on animals.

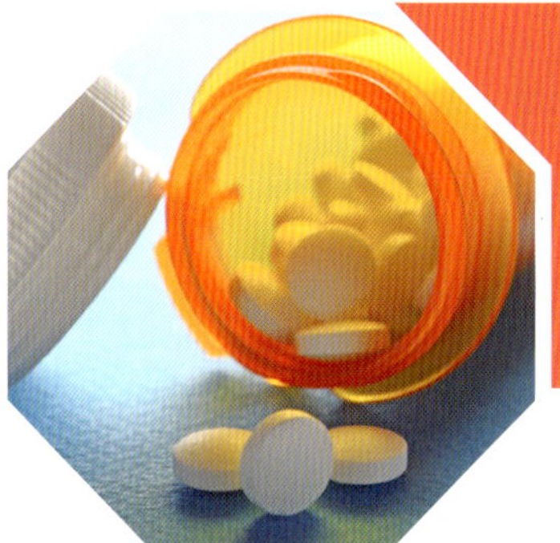

The United States imports medical supplies from more than **150** foreign countries. Most of those countries have different medical standards than the United States.

FDA Today

The FDA works to keep up with a changing world. New technology offers advances in medicine. However, it also offers challenges. There are many new medicines and products to be tested before they can be released to the public. The number of products that must be tested by the FDA increases every year.

Today, the FDA is also involved in preventing terrorist attacks. There is a worry that terrorists could use food or medicine to attack a large group of people. To fight this, the FDA is working closely with the DHS. Together, they are closely watching the food and drugs that are imported into the United States. This is one of the many reasons why the FDA has opened offices around the world.

Globalization is also placing new strains on the FDA. The world's countries are doing business with each other more than ever before. This helps the U.S. economy. However, because so many countries want to do business with the United States, this also makes it a challenge to make sure products from all over the world are safe. There are not enough FDA inspectors.

93 percent of all seafood consumed in the United States is imported from other countries. The FDA is responsible for inspecting it all.

Tobacco

MODERN CASE STUDY

Harvey Wiley was ahead of his time. In 1927, when most people used tobacco, Wiley wrote that he felt that it was not safe. He thought it might even cause cancer. The FDA fought for many years to force tobacco companies to warn users that their product might be dangerous to their health. In 1965, the FDA won. For the first time, tobacco companies had to put a warning label on the packages.

However, both sides continued to struggle. The FDA wanted the industry to admit it added chemicals to cigarettes. These made them more addictive. However, the industry denied it. Finally, secret talks between tobacco industry leaders were leaked. They proved that they had been lying to the public for years.

Today the use of tobacco is still legal. However, the tobacco industry must warn that the use of tobacco can cause cancer. People under the age of 18 cannot purchase it. Where people can smoke has also been greatly limited. People still have their right to choose, but they must know the choice they are making.

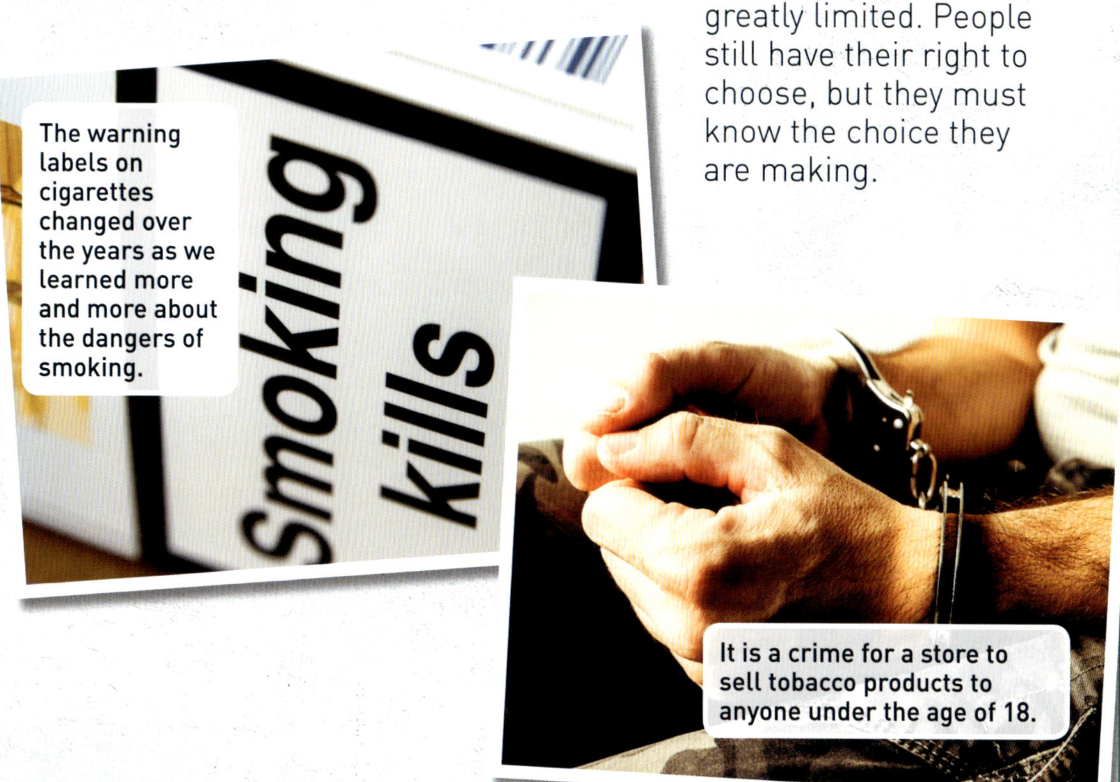

The warning labels on cigarettes changed over the years as we learned more and more about the dangers of smoking.

It is a crime for a store to sell tobacco products to anyone under the age of 18.

FDA Looking to the Future

Today's FDA must plan for tomorrow's threats. This planning can be difficult. Both technology and U.S. culture are changing.

One of the biggest threats the FDA faces in the future is medical terrorism. This is not new. In early 1982, in Chicago, the United States saw its first case of medical terrorism. Someone mixed the pain reliever Tylenol with the deadly poison cyanide. The bottles looked exactly the same. Seven people died.

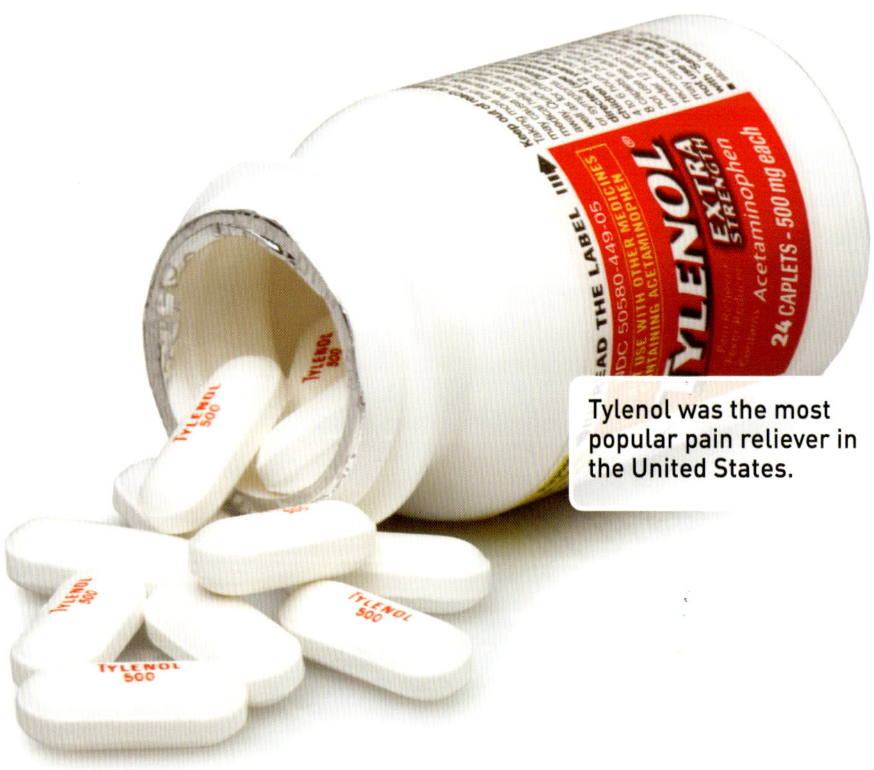

Tylenol was the most popular pain reliever in the United States.

The FDA is working hard to make sure such an attack does not happen again. Planning for the future means that the FDA must keep up with all of the different ways that medical terrorism could be done using new technology.

Every day, we also learn more about the human body and how it works. A drug or medical device that was approved by the FDA ten years ago might be a bad drug tomorrow. The FDA must know about every medical breakthrough that happens as soon as it happens.

The technology used in medical procedures is changing rapidly. Whole operations are now done by robots instead of human hands. The FDA must have many different technical specialists that understand the lasers, computers, robots, and other new tools that are being created all over the world for use in the medical field.

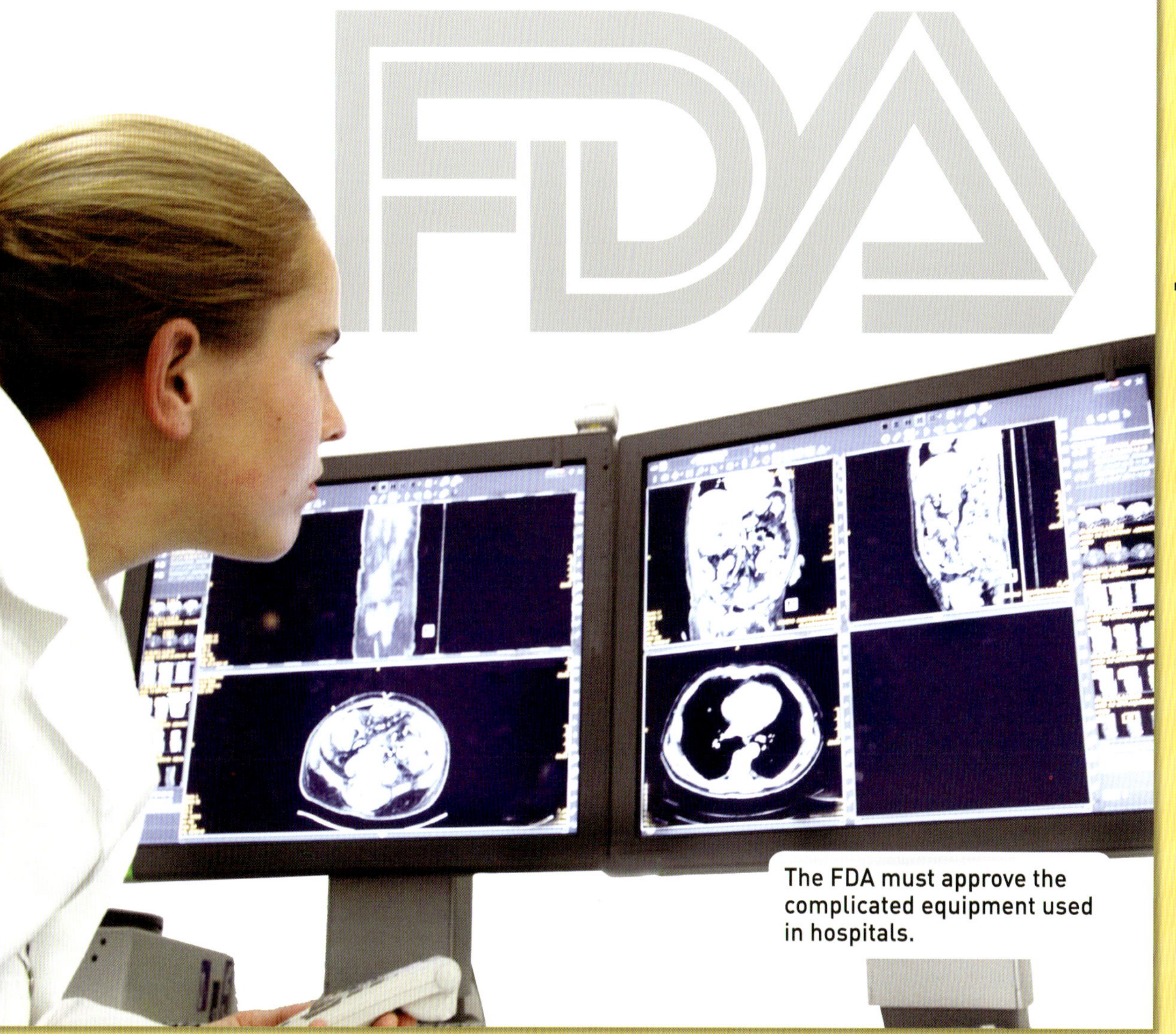

The FDA must approve the complicated equipment used in hospitals.

ACTIVITY ★★

Create a Policy Paper

Rather than go on a diet, it is better to eat healthy food. However, there are so many tasty snacks out there it can be hard to say "no." It is important for the FDA to tell people what foods might be bad for them, while also allowing U.S. citizens to make their own choices.

The FDA has made several food products illegal. But what about your freedom of choice? The Preamble to the Constitution says that it is the job of the government to "promote the general welfare." That means to help keep us healthy.

Develop your own thoughts about what parts of your diet and the foods you eat the federal government should be able to regulate, if any. Write a policy paper that summarizes your opinion.

Step 1:

Answer the following questions to help you develop your opinion.

1. Should the FDA be able to outlaw foods that we know to be unhealthy? If not, why not?
2. Should people be allowed to consume poison? If not, why not?
3. If a government does not control the safety of its food, is it putting its citizens lives in danger?
4. Does the United States have the right to force its citizens to not eat foods that are unhealthy? If not, why not?
5. Are there any reasons why a U.S. citizen should be forced to eat something that is known to be healthy? If yes, why?
6. Are there any reasons why the government should make you eat a totally healthy diet? If yes, why?
7. Does the United States have the right to decide what time of year foods are available?

Step 2:

Take your opinions from Question 1 - 7 and write a one-page policy paper. It should explain the policy you think is correct about how much government should be allowed to regulate its citizens' diet and the snacks they eat, if any. It should also explain why. Include an introductory paragraph.

- Paragraph 1: What is the question?
- Paragraph 2: What are the issues surrounding the question?
- Paragraph 3: What is your policy on the issue, and why?

QUIZ ★★

1 What was today's FDA called when it first started in 1906?

2 Who was the commissioner in 1906 of what would become the FDA?

3 Who was the first female commissioner of the FDA?

4 How old do you need to be to purchase a tobacco product?

5 What do the initials FDA stand for?

6 What are the main products the FDA regulates?

7 What agency did the FDA work with after a 1937 mass poisoning in Tennessee?

8 What was the drug that FDA doctor Frances Kelley helped prevent from reaching the United States?

9 Which industry did the FDA force to put warning labels on its packaging?

10 Where did the first case of medical terrorism occur in the United States?

ANSWERS

1. Bureau of Chemistry 2. Harvey Wiley 3. Jane Henney 4. Eighteen 5. Food and Drug Administration 6. Food, Drugs, Medical equipment, Cosmetics, and Tobacco 7. FBI 8. Thalidomide 9. Tobacco industry 10. Chicago

KEY WORDS

bacterial: relating to or caused by bacteria. Bacteria are single-celled organisms.

checks and balances: Counterbalancing influences by which a system is regulated.

civil liberties: individual rights protected by law

conflict of interests: situations in which serving one interest could involve working against another

Congress: governing body consisting of two chambers, the House of Representatives and the Senate

Constitution: the supreme law of the United States of America

cosmetic products: skin moisturizers, perfumes, lipsticks, shampoos, and deodorants

ecological: the relation of living organisms to one another and to their environment

Eighteenth Amendment: this amendment banned the sale and drinking of alcohol in the United States. It is the only amendment to be repealed from the constitution.

globalization: the process by which organizations start operating on an international scale

overreach: to go above or beyond

pharmaceutical: relating to the use and sale of medicinal drugs

popular sovereignty: the idea that the authority of a state and its government are controlled by the people of the state

regulations: a rule or order issued by a regulatory agency of the government

repealed: removed or reversed a law

toxic: poisonous

veterinary medicine: the branch of medicine that deals with the care of animals

INDEX

LIGHTBOX

SUPPLEMENTARY RESOURCES

Click on the plus icon found in the bottom left corner of each spread to open additional teacher resources.

- Download and print the book's quizzes and activities
- Access curriculum correlations
- Explore additional web applications that enhance the Lightbox experience

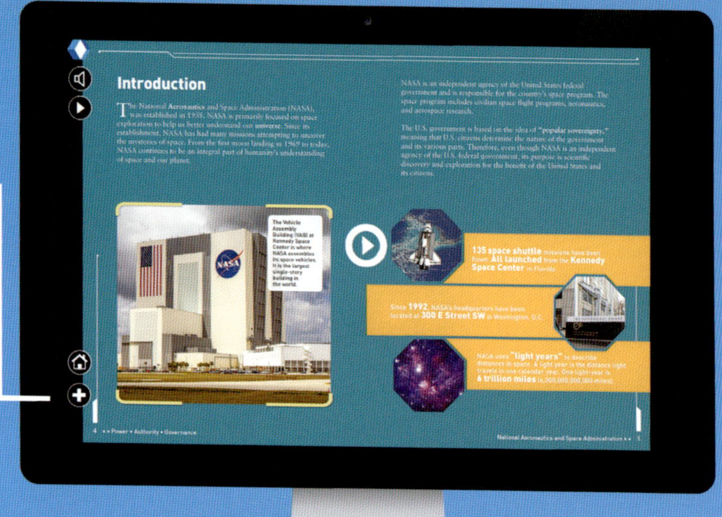

LIGHTBOX DIGITAL TITLES

Packed full of integrated media

VIDEOS

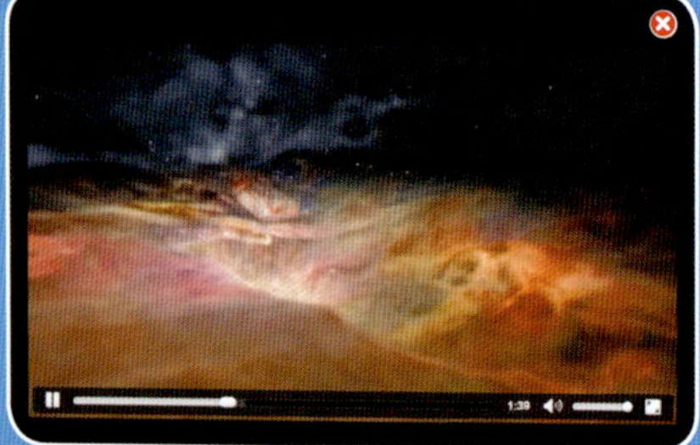

INTERACTIVE MAPS

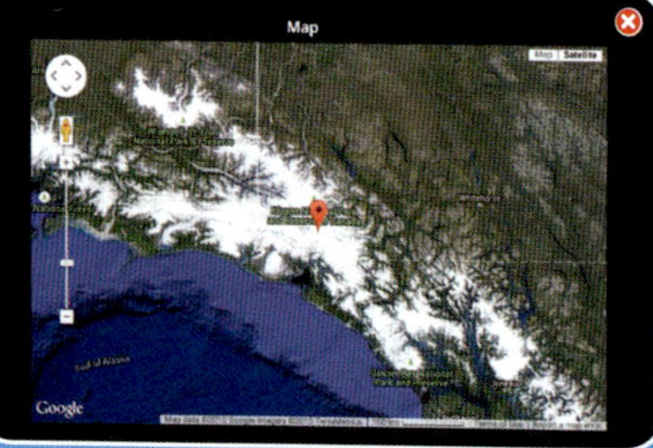

WEBLINKS

SLIDESHOWS

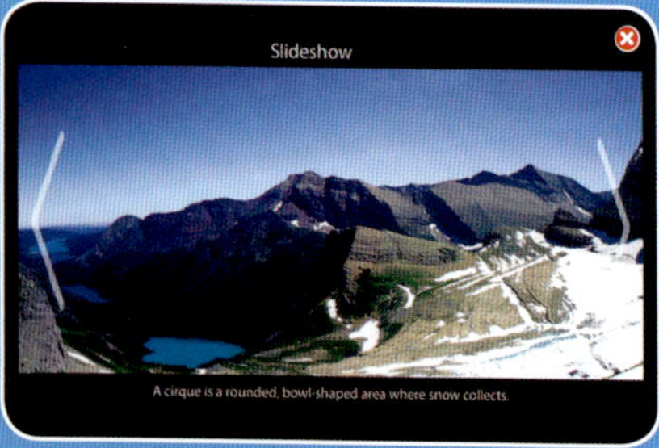

A cirque is a rounded, bowl-shaped area where snow collects.

QUIZZES

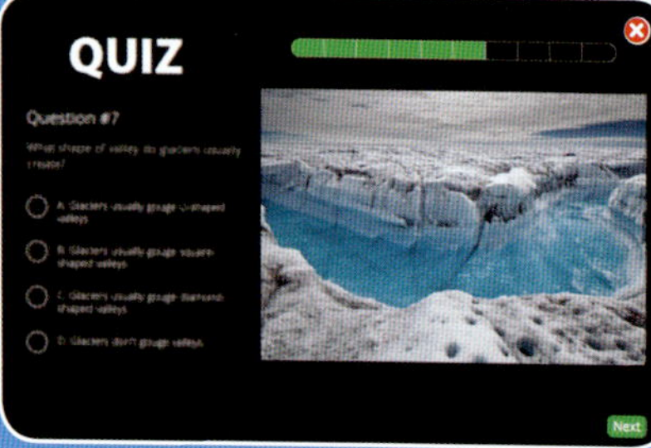

OPTIMIZED FOR
- ✓ TABLETS
- ✓ WHITEBOARDS
- ✓ COMPUTERS
- ✓ AND MUCH MORE!

Published by Smartbook Media Inc.
350 5th Avenue, 59th Floor New York, NY 10118
Website: www.openlightbox.com

Library of Congress Control Number: 2019939792

ISBN 978-1-5105-4677-6 (hardcover)
ISBN 978-1-5105-4678-3 (multi-user eBook)

Printed in Guangzhou, China
1 2 3 4 5 6 7 8 9 0 23 22 21 20 19

052019
122718

Editor: John Willis
Art Director: Terry Paulhus

Every reasonable effort has been made to trace ownership and to obtain permission to reprint copyright material. The publisher would be pleased to have any errors or omissions brought to its attention so that they may be corrected in subsequent printings.

The publisher acknowledges Alamy, Shutterstock, and Wikimedia Commons as its primary image suppliers for this title.